21 Days to Improved Mental Well-Being

Dr. Mel Tavares

(C) 2023 Mel Tavares

Published by Simply Right Press

All rights reserved. This book or any portion thereof may not be reproduced or used in any manner whatsoever without the express written permission of the author except for the use of brief quotations in a book review.

Scriptures marked AMP are taken from the AMPLIFIED BIBLE (AMP): Scripture taken from the AMPLIFIED® BIBLE, Copyright © 1954, 1958, 1962, 1964, 1965, 1987 by the Lockman Foundation Used by Permission.

Scriptures marked NLT are taken from the HOLY BIBLE, NEW LIVING TRANSLATION (NLT): Scriptures taken from the HOLY BIBLE, NEW LIVING TRANSLATION, Copyright© 1996, 2004, 2007 by Tyndale House Foundation. Used by permission of Tyndale House Publishers, Inc., Carol Stream, Illinois 60188. All rights reserved. Used by permission.

Scriptures marked KJV are taken from the KING JAMES VERSION (KJV): KING JAMES VERSION, public domain.

Scriptures marked NAS are taken from the NEW AMERICAN STANDARD (NAS): Scripture taken from the NEW AMERICAN STANDARD BIBLE®, copyright© 1960, 1962, 1963, 1968, 1971, 1972, 1973, 1975, 1977, 1995 by The Lockman Foundation. Used by permission.

Scriptures marked NIV are taken from the NEW INTERNATIONAL VERSION (NIV): Scripture taken from THE HOLY BIBLE, NEW INTERNATIONAL VERSION ®. Copyright© 1973, 1978, 1984, 2011 by Biblica, Inc.™. Used by permission of Zondervan

Scriptures marked ESV are taken from the THE HOLY BIBLE, ENGLISH STANDARD VERSION (ESV): Scriptures taken from THE HOLY BIBLE, ENGLISH STANDARD VERSION ® Copyright© 2001 by Crossway, a publishing ministry of Good News Publishers. Used by permission. Scriptures marked TLB are taken from the THE LIVING BIBLE (TLB): Scripture taken from THE LIVING BIBLE copyright© 1971. Used by permission of Tyndale House Publishers, Inc., Carol Stream, Illinois 60188. All rights reserved.

Scriptures marked TM are taken from the THE MESSAGE: THE BIBLE IN CONTEMPORARY ENGLISH (TM): Scripture taken from THE MESSAGE: THE BIBLE IN CONTEMPORARY ENGLISH, copyright©1993, 1994, 1995, 1996, 2000, 2001, 2002. Used by permission of NavPress Publishing Group

About the Author

Mel Tavares is an accomplished award-winning author, speaker/teacher, counselor and coach both in ministry and in her career.

She has invested 40 years in counseling women in the secular and church settings, focusing primarily on women needing hope and healing. Mel holds a Doctorate of Ministry, works in the Pastoral Care and Counseling Department at her church, is a member of the AACC (American Association of Christian Counselors), AWSA (Advanced Writers and Speakers Association), and is the founder of Kingdom Writers, the Connecticut Chapter of the ACW (American Christian Writers).

In addition to ghostwriting and authoring her books, Mel is a contributing author to several books and writes for multiple online Christian communities. She is a member of the Word of Life Youth Ministries writing team and rejoices in the curriculum reaching youth in over 80 countries. She teaches digitally and in person, conducts Facebook Live series, and is a frequent media guest. Mel is a wife, mom to seven, and grandma to ten. Contact info can be found @ drmeltavares.com

21 Days to Improved Mental Well-Being

This collection of encouraging daily devotions is written for all who desire improvement in their mental well-being. At various points in our lives, we all face struggles and challenges threatening our mental health. This book is designed to serve as a resource and reminder to you of ways to improve your mental well-being immediately. For the next 21 days, commit to slowly and thoughtfully reading the following pages. As you do so, pray for God to show you the application for your life. May you find healing and improved mental well-being.

Disclaimer: This book is intended to be a tool, not a replacement for mental health counseling or coaching. It is not the intent of the author that a person with a clinical diagnosis or prescribed medication would use this book for anything other than to augment the care you are receiving.

If you are experiencing acute mental health symptoms or are considering suicide, please immediately call or text 988 or go to the website to confidentially chat: https://988lifeline.org/?utm_source=google&utm_medium=web&utm_campaign=onebox

21 Days to Improved Mental Well-Being

Table of Contents

Front Matter

Pg. 1   Day 1   Lord, I Need Rest

Pg. 4   Day 2   Listen for the Still Voice Above the Noise

Pg.7   Day 3   The Art of Self-Care

Pg.10   Day 4   The Resurrected King is Resurrecting You

Pg.13   Day 5   You Can Trust God's Character

Pg.16   Day 6   Overcoming Loneliness

Pg. 19   Day 7   Seasonal Changes Can Affect You

Pg.22   Day 8   From Dormancy to Bloom

Pg.25   Day 9   Perspective in a World Filled with Evil

Pg.28   Day 10   Let Go of Past Mistakes

Pg.32   Day 11   Never Too Late, Never Too Old

Pg.35   Day 12   Reaching and Setting Goals

Pg. 38   Day 13   Discover Your Purpose of Life on Earth

Pg.42   Day 14   Believe God Will Help You

Pg.45   Day 15 Defeat Financial Anxieties

Pg. 49 Day 16 Hope When Not with Your Loved One

Pg. 52 Day 17 Coping During the Holidays

Pg. 56 Day 18 Choose Kindness Over Bitterness

Pg. 60 Day 19 Trust in the Faithfulness of Jesus

Pg. 63 Day 20 God Wants to Forgive You

Pg. 67 Day 21 Be Thankful in All Things

Bonus Materials
Top Questions People Suffering Anxiety Ask

Pg.72 #1 Do I Have to Clean Up My Act First?

Pg.75 #2 Why Is There So Much Evil in the World?

Pg.77 #3 Is There Life After Death?

Pg.82 #4 Why Do Christians Read the Bible So Much?

Pg.86 #5. Can a Christian Enjoy Entertainment?

Pg.90 #6. How Should I Pray for Healing?

Back Matter

Pg.94 Resources
Pg.96 Additional Works by Dr. Mel Tavares

~1~

Lord, I Need Some Rest

Mark 1:35 (NIV) *"Very early in the morning when it was still dark, Jesus got up, left the house, and went to a solitary place, where he prayed."*

Too often, I find myself breathing a quick prayer heavenward that sounds something like, "Lord, I need some rest. I'm doing all of this work in your name and for Your glory, but people keep coming with their needs. I'm so tired."

Jesus spent his days in ministry just as I do while working at my church. People surrounded him everywhere he went, yet he never seemed to run out of the energy to minister to someone in need. A leper, a blind man, a woman with an issue of blood, a demon-possessed man. How is it that Jesus never seemed to tire?

I'm learning to follow the example of Jesus. Jesus knew the day would be busy from the time the household awoke and would not be denied time in prayer with his Father. Prayer and communion with our Heavenly Father allow us to enter spiritual rest.

In his case, Jesus left the house and found a solitary place where he would not be disturbed. While striving to follow Jesus' example of waking early enough to spend time with the Father before my busy day begins, I confess that I do not get up when it is still dark. My respect to all who are early risers. I set my alarm for an hour earlier than necessary to get ready for work, make coffee and eagerly make my way to my favorite chair on the porch to spend time with the Lord.

Although Mark 1:35 does not explicitly say that Jesus slept during the night, nighttime sleep is inferred by the phrase, "*Jesus got up and left the house.*" If he got up, he was likely getting up from a night of sleep.

Science agrees with the example Jesus demonstrated of our need for physical rest. Sleep is restorative for our minds and bodies. I've tried drinking more caffeine and sleeping less, but cups of coffee leave me bleary-eyed and brain-fogged the next day. There is no replacement for a solid eight hours of sleep that rejuvenates and prepares us for the tasks awaiting us the following day.

I look forward to Saturdays. It is my down day, my Sabbath, as I am actively involved in our Sunday church services. It's a time for family gatherings, trips to the beach, and date nights with my hubby. I guard these days and rarely allow the endless opportunities to engage in other activities to infringe on this day of rest. I have learned that mini periods of rest throughout the week are adequate for several days in a row, but God gave us the example of working six days and resting on the seventh. Whatever your schedule, I pray you prioritize a day of rest each week.

At first glance, it may seem that morning quiet time and afternoon breaks on the porch allow the brain to rest, and a whole night of restorative sleep and an entire day a week off is enough rest. I have found I also need extended periods, and I intentionally schedule a few days to a week off several times a year. During those extended periods of rest, I unplug. I don't take my laptop, avoid social media, and put an auto-responder on my email.

Admittedly, it is hard to withdraw from the pressing needs of those I serve daily. I have learned from Jesus that there will always be people who need us, and as difficult as it is, we must take daily and weekly time to rest, and I am convinced He would approve occasional vacations.

Prayer: *"Jesus, thank you for showing me how and when to rest. Thank you for making provisions for my weary body and soul to be restored and rejuvenated. I ask that you continue teaching me how to continue learning to rest when I need it."*

~2~
Listen for the Still Voice above the Noise

John 10:4 (NIV) *"When he has brought out all his own, he goes on ahead of them, and his sheep follow him because they know his voice."*

God speaks to people every day and desires for you to also hear His voice when He speaks. There is no magic formula to hearing His voice. He speaks in many ways, including in your mind, through chapters you read in the Bible, and through conversations with other people. At times, He speaks through dreams or visions. The issue is that we live in a noisy world and are often too busy to listen or haven't developed the ability to recognize His voice.

God speaks to your mind, but you may interpret His voice as your own thought because you don't recognize His voice. Although some people report hearing an audible voice of God, more often, it will be a 'still, small voice' you will hear. He desires to communicate with you throughout your days, much the same as if you were communicating with a friend or spouse.

When you read the Bible or pray, thoughts will enter your mind. The more connected you are to Him, conversing throughout the day, the more easily you will recognize that He is talking to you.

God uses other Christians to speak to you. You may have been seeking an answer from God about a specific situation and later converse with another Christian. You may bring up the situation, and the other person will give wise counsel. Did you know that God may speak to you through the other person? You may be with the person who may speak to you and randomly talk about a Bible verse or a life principle that gives the exact answer you were looking for. Rest assured it was no coincidence; God is providing the answer for you if you have an ear to hear.

There are times when God uses dramatic means to get our attention. If you are not in close communication with Him and not listening for His voice, God will speak to you through financial insecurities, housing insecurities, employment struggles, relational problems, and more. How often do we cry out to God when we encounter hard times? It is during a crisis that many open their ears, desperate to hear from God if only to get the answer to "Why is this happening?"

The importance of recognizing God's voice cannot be overstated. You must learn to hear God's voice if you want answers to your questions and prayers. He can and does speak to you, but you must recognize His voice and discern that it is God, not Satan or your thoughts or the well-meaning input of strangers.

Just one word from God can change everything. Sometimes it is one word; sometimes, it is an ongoing conversation God has with us. The important thing is that we don't miss His voice. The voice of God speaking can transform your marriage, give you the direction you seek about finances, speak to your illness and heal your disease, or give insight into a complex situation at your job.

Prayer: *"Dear God, teach me to recognize your voice. You are the shepherd, and I know you give your sheep answers, direction, and guidance each day. I am listening."*

~3~
The Art of Self-Care

Luke 4:42 (ESV) says, *"And went it was day, he departed and went to a desolate place."*

Have you ever been so mentally exhausted that your brain seemingly stops processing? That happened to me recently, at the end of a hectic season of life. After pushing through project after project, I hit the proverbial wall. I told my husband I was "Crispy, fried, overcooked, done and I need a day at the beach." I secretly thought I needed a week at the beach but figured a day would allow me to recharge.

For me, the beach is where I recharge. Your recharging station may be a park or a mountain filled with hiking trails. We all need a place to retreat that is void of noise and distractions and will allow us to spend extended time with the Lord.

Uniquely created, God knows my innermost being and understands the beach is where I listen most intently to Him. "Meet me at the beach," He whispered.

The next day I packed my beach bag, excited as I thought about an entire day of resting and communing with the Lord. I packed a journal, pen, Bible, favorite devotional, sunscreen, water bottles, and snacks.

Driving to the beach, I thought of Jesus and His frequent withdrawal from ministering to people so he could pray. As reports of Jesus' miracles spread, crowds increasingly followed him. Luke 16 (ESV) says, *"But, he would withdraw to desolate places and pray."* Mark 1:36 (ESV) gives a similar account. *"And rising very early in the morning, while it was still dark, he departed to a desolate place, and there he prayed."*

If Jesus frequently needed to stop ministering to people and withdraw to a quiet place to pray, the same need is true for us. My mistake over the past couple of months is that I momentarily forgot the importance of frequently withdrawing and pushed myself too hard. What about you? Do you remember to stop and retreat to a quiet place, to recharge?

My day at the beach was wonderful. I sat and observed all the Lord had created, and praise poured out of my mind and into my journal. I wrote as the Lord spoke words of direction and encouragement.

As I let waves of the Holy Spirit refreshing crash over me, I felt strength arising. I thought about the timing of Jesus' withdrawals and how often he withdrew before or after pouring himself out: After he multiplied the loaves and fishes (Mark 6:46), before he chose his disciples (Luke 6:12), and before the transfiguration (Luke 9:28). As I reflected on these truths, my emotions normalized, realizing if Jesus needed to experience the ebb and flow of withdrawing and ministering; certainly, it is normal for me to need the same pattern.

As the waning sun shimmered with hues of orange and pink on the water, joy returned to my soul. Not that I had been anxious or depressed, but the weariness of ministry with no breaks had depleted my emotions. Reluctantly, I packed my things and made my way to my car. As I drove back to the city that never sleeps, where addicts roam the streets and trafficked women lurk in the shadows, I felt the weight of ministry needs descending.

Is there a lifestyle change you need to make to enable you to withdraw to a quiet place? Do you need to get up earlier, before your household? Do you need to carve out time to sit by the water or walk in the garden in the cool of the night as you commune with the Lord?

Prayer: *"Dear God, thank you for your beautiful creation you've given for us to enjoy. Teach me the value of taking a day to practice self-care and get outside in the fresh air. Thank you for showing me the necessity of taking time to recharge frequently."*

~4~
The Resurrected King is Resurrecting You

Luke 24:34 (NAS) *"The Lord is really risen and appeared to Simon."*

There are more than 100 verses in the Bible that speak of Jesus being resurrected, having risen from the grave in bodily form. All hail King Jesus, all hail Emmanuel! He's the King of Kings and Lord of Lords!

Jesus is the Resurrected King. If we will bow to the one who wore our sin and shame with a crown of thorns, He will do the miraculous for us. Do you need a miracle this week? Are you in need of resurrection?

Do you know that He can resurrect you from your circumstances and feelings? Like Job of the Bible, who was resurrected from the ash pile of despair, like the dry bones resurrected in the valley of death, like the son of the widow resurrected from the dead, the Lord Jesus is continually resurrecting those who cry out to Him.

Many people are feeling defeated and in despair. Media reports generate a continual picture of doom and gloom causing fear of the future. Officials would have citizens believe initiatives will be the savior for those facing financial ruin, yet many find they do not qualify for the help they desperately need in the midst of inflation at a 40-year high. Grief and sorrow threaten to swallow any shadow of hope left in the wake of a three-year stretch like none other in the last hundred years. And now, there are wars and rumors of war at an increased level. We need a better savior, a better rescue plan than what the world can offer us.

Jesus is that Savior, capital S. He is the Rescue Plan. He is the one who pulls us up from the ashes of defeat and allows us to have a hope that is found in the eternal truths of the Bible, not the circumstances of this world.

If you know Him, rise up in Resurrection Power! The three days between crucifixion and resurrection were for you! He fought the battle, stormed the gates of hell, and took the keys of death for you! He did it for you; believe that! The work is finished. It is your choice to believe and apprehend all He has done for you!

The Bible is filled with promises given to us of a hope and a future. His eye is on the sparrow. You will be taken care of. His plans for you are good. You can be sure that the work He has started in you will be finished. Stand firm on the promise that He will work all things together for your ultimate good. He who owns the cattle on a thousand hills is more than able to meet your needs. He can heal your disease. He can restore fractured relationships. Lift up your voice and give a shout of praise to Jesus because your

Resurrected King wants to resurrect you, restore you, and reconcile you!

The Resurrected King is resurrecting me. He is no respecter of persons. What He's doing for me, He will do for you. Don't let another day go by sitting on the ash pile of despair and hopelessness. Rise up, rise up! Ask Jesus to resurrect your situation and turn it into good! It's Resurrection Day for you, just as it was for Jesus over two thousand years ago!

Prayer: *"Dear God, thank you for sending your son Jesus. Thank you, Jesus, for dying on the cross and rising again as our Resurrected King. I ask that you help me rise up from the ashes of my circumstances in the Resurrection Power you have provided."*

~5~
You Can Trust God's Character

Exodus 3:14 (NASB) "*God said to Moses, 'I AM WHO I AM'; and He said, 'Thus you shall say to the sons of Israel, I AM has sent me to you'*"

When hard times hit, and you find yourself questioning why something has happened, set your mind on the character of God. Remembering His character will help you to stay calm and steady amid your situation.

God is the great I AM.

He is eternal and unchanging. Remember that He loves you with an everlasting love. He allows nothing and does nothing that is not intended for your good. Romans 8:28 (NIV) says, "*And we know that in all things, God works for the good of those who love Him and are called according to His purpose.*"

"How could a loving God allow a loved one to be estranged from me?" I have often been asked. "Why would God let my company lay me off after ten years? How is that a part of His plan?" "How will God bring something good out of my husband cheating on me?" While listening and providing counsel, I hear the heart cry of women in pain.

It has been my experience that most of the time, God typically helps me see the purpose in due season. He doesn't have to explain anything to us, but many times he has graciously allowed me insight and understanding. If a family member is estranged because of a difference in values and beliefs, the Lord may allow it for a season for the purpose of working in the heart of your estranged family member. A job lay-off may be paving the way for redirection into a job better aligned with your gifts and calling.

When answers to our questions don't come, it is important to trust God. Psalm 146: 3-4 is a great passage that reinforces reasons why God is trustworthy. Give thanks to the Lord of lords. His love endures forever. To him who alone does great wonders, His love endures forever.

When struggling to find someone or something to trust, indeed, God is the only one deemed trustworthy enough to be with us through our journey in this life. Earthly fathers, family, friends, and organizations, even Pastors and church family fail us. Not intentionally, but life gets in the way. Misunderstandings happen. People get frustrated or fatigued, and they fail us. The Bible is filled with the promises of God, who is trustworthy because in His perfection, cannot fail to keep the promises He has made.

It is not in the character of God to plan anything less than what is best for you as His beloved child. He formed you in your mother's womb, and before you were formed, He knew the plans for your life. Because He is unchanging, it is impossible for Him to change His plans for you. The free will of man may have changed circumstances in your life (EG a job, housing situation, etc.). The free will of a loved one may have caused them to overdose and pass away. Those were not the plan of God for you, but free will entered in. Even so, God is not surprised about the choices others make that impact your life.

When in doubt, think back to all the ways God has blessed you and provided for you over your life. His unchanging (Immutable) character means those traits you've experienced before can be depended on now, in your current situation. Storms will come and go, circumstances will swirl around you, but you can trust and put your faith in the omniscience (all-knowing) character of God.

Prayer: *"Dear God, thank you for always being trustworthy. I know that you love me and you have plans for me. Help me to trust you when bad things happen in my life and to have the courage to walk through difficult times."*

~6~
Overcoming Loneliness

Isaiah 58:11 (NLV) *The Lord will always lead you. He will meet the needs of your soul in the dry times and give strength to your body. You will be like a garden that has enough water, like a well of water that never dries up.*

We all experience loneliness from time to time. Nothing has caused more loneliness than the recent pandemic we found ourselves living through. The result for many was a complete feeling of disconnect and loneliness. For some, loneliness remains a constant companion in the wake of loss and grief.

Loneliness can make people feel empty, unwanted, and alone. As loneliness increases, the risk for depression increases. We begin to wonder why we are here on earth, what our purpose is, and question God in the midst of it.

God is still right where He's always been. Sometimes we don't feel His presence because we 'break fellowship' and don't seek him out. Isaiah 58:11 says when you seek Him you will find that your soul will begin to feel less parched and dry. The longer we spend with the Lord each day, the more the waters will flow and the garden of our soul will flourish.

While a person may crave human contact, the state of mind may make it difficult to form connections. We are created to need each other, but if loneliness sets in, making an effort to go to church can be overwhelming.

Loneliness and isolation can lead to health complications if left unresolved. Loneliness becomes a higher risk factor the older a person gets. A sedentary lifestyle coupled with poor nutrition leads to physical disease. Take action and implement some practical tips to overcome loneliness and allow your soul to flourish like the well-watered garden our Lord desires you to experience.

Three Tips for Overcoming Loneliness

1. Create a daily schedule and try to stick to it. Although it may seem meaningless, especially if you are not working, it really will help! Be sure to include one task a day that is a priority, so there is a feeling of accomplishment and a decrease in feeling lonely.

2. Connect with God and others. Communing with the Lord each day will water your soul but it is not enough to sustain you because we are created to be in fellowship with others too. If you are not in a small group in a local church, I urge you to join one. It is in the small groups that we are best connected on a personal level. Just attending church services but not really getting to know people will leave your soul

barren. Step out of your comfort zone and force yourself to be with others. Your soul will thank you.

3. Eat healthy and nutritious foods. Overly processed foods contain chemicals that suppress your 'joy meter.' When you feel healthier physically, your emotions will improve, and loneliness will decrease. In addition to eating healthy, you need to stay active. If you are unable to leave your home, check out YouTube Walk-at-Home videos. If at all possible, get outside and be active. You will see people and at least be able to exchange a 'hello' and know you are a part of the outdoor community.

Prayer: *"Dear God, thank you for being with me all of my days. Help me to take action and implement some ideas of how to decrease my feelings of loneliness, including connecting me to others."*

~7~
Seasonal Changes Can Affect You

Genesis 8:22 (ESV) says, *"While the earth remains, seedtime and harvest, cold and heat, summer and winter, day and night, shall not cease."*

God created this beautiful earth for us to enjoy, and for centuries, people have spent the majority of their days being active outside. Today, many of us are relegated to office settings and miss the benefits of being in the sunlight for several hours a day. This creates a deficit spiritually and mentally.

While most people associate Seasonal Affective Disorder (SAD) with the winter months, the truth is the changing of any season can trigger symptoms. This is especially true when summer draws to a close, and the sun begins to set earlier in the day. Less daylight can cause feelings of sadness, sluggishness, and generalized depression. While some are impacted to the degree of being diagnosed, more than 10 million people experience at least some level of struggle with seasonal changes, and women are four times more likely to than men.

I drink my coffee and have my quiet time in the morning most days, even in the winter. Sometimes I have to force myself to put on my wool jacket and just go sit in the fresh air and sunshine because I know how important it is for my overall health. As I sip my coffee, I listen to all creatures, great and small, and marvel at the handiwork of the Lord, including the beauty of the trees in each season.

Being alone with the Lord is essential but it is also important to be in fellowship with other Christians. The Bible is filled with verses that speak to the need to be together, including 1 Thessalonians 5:11 (ESV) which reminds us to *"Encourage one another and build one another up"* When we encourage someone, we are building them up in a way that allows them to continue in the work of the ministry.

Hebrews 10:25 (ESV) speaks to the need to meet together, all the more as we see the Day drawing near. *"'Not neglecting to meet together, as is the habit of some, but encouraging one another, and all the more as you see the Day drawing near."* We know the enemy is wreaking havoc in the world; therefore, we need other believers.

God created us to walk together, bearing one another's burdens (Galatians 6:2) and spurring each other on as we journey forward. Romans 1:12 (ESV) points us to the reason God calls us to walk together *"that we may be mutually encouraged by each other's faith, both yours and mine."* When there are practical or spiritual needs, we are there to pray for one another and to meet the needs in various ways. Fight the tendency to isolate and be intentional about being with others for their benefit and for your own.

Seasons change as surely as the sun rises and sets. You may struggle as literal or spiritual seasons change, including as summer fades to fall. Eating healthy, exercising daily, spending time outside each day, fellowshipping with other people, and getting the right amount of sleep each night will work together to lessen the impact on your mental, physical, and spiritual health. I pray blessings over you in this next season of your life!

Prayer: *'Dear God, thank you for the wonderful creatures and plants you have given me to enjoy. Thank you for the changes in seasons, both spiritually and in the earth. Teach me to be proactive in combating seasonal changes' impact on me."*

~8~
From Dormancy to Bloom

Matthew 11:28 (NASB) *"Come to me, all you who are weary and heavy-laden, and I will give you rest."*

There is power in the dormancy of winter, which bursts forth as new growth in the spring. Have you ever looked at deciduous trees in the winter and thought about how dead they look? There are no leaves, no blooms, and seemingly no life left in the tree. Yet beneath the surface, new growth is happening. As surely as night turns to day, my dead-looking apple tree bursts forth into bloom every spring. Every spring, I marvel at the beauty of the blooms budding from the seemingly lifeless tree and then at the fruit that begins to grow out of the once cold, grey branches.

The same concept is true of perennial plants. This morning I walked past my daffodil bed. There's no evidence of life in the flower bed, as all the bulbs lay dormant. If I didn't know about the power of dormancy, I would have dug up the seemingly dead bulbs and thrown them out last summer after they stopped blooming. Because I have a background in horticulture, I know there is life in the bulbs, but they went into a period of dormancy to protect themselves from the stressors of the environment and the impact on them.

God gives us rest in seasons of dormancy. A person may look at you and think there is little going on in your life and you are not being fruitful in the Kingdom. Spiritually mature people will recognize God's work in their life beneath the surface in preparation for the next season in their life.

At some point, like plants, many of us go into 'survival mode.' If you've experienced it, you know what I am talking about. Trying to keep up with the day-to-day becomes too much. I tend to 'shut down' emotionally first. I can physically cook, clean, and work but cannot handle the emotional and mental fatigue. My psyche goes into a state of dormancy. Can you relate to this?

Oftentimes, the Lord will call us to a time of dormancy before moving us into the next level and season of life. While others may question your well-being if they observe your withdrawal from activities and interactions, know there is power in the time of dormancy. Explain if you must, but don't feel guilty about stopping for a time.

When plants are in a state of dormancy, the foliage and blooms cease growing, but the roots are still alive and growing. The same is true when we withdraw and power down for a while. During this season, growth occurs deep in our spiritual roots as we dwell in the presence of the Lord, listen to worship music, read the Bible, and are introspective.

Emerging from your season of dormancy should be a gradual process. Leave room for the emotional and mental stressors that will continue to come your way, and schedule in time for rest and relaxation. These measures will allow the fruit of your life to bloom once again. Until then, remember that your time of dormancy is not in vain. Growth is still happening, and you are being recharged and rejuvenated; when you emerge, you will be powerful and effective in ministering to your family and those around you.

Prayer: *"Lord, thank you for teaching me the value of a quiet, seemingly dormant season. Help me to rest in your presence as you prepare me for the next season of life."*

~9~

Perspective in a World Filled with Evil

John 14:1 (NIV) *"Do not let your hearts be troubled. You believe in God; believe also in me."*

We are living in a world filled with all sorts of evil, including crime, war, terrorism, racism, and all manner of societal woes. The snowball effect occurs as evil happens and incites yet another act of evil and hatred. As things intensify, many are asking why evil is in the world. For some, it causes feelings of hopelessness and despair. If you are feeling this way, know there is hope. Please read on.

Evil exists in the world because of two primary sources. The devil (referred to as Satan hereafter) is a primary source and has free reign to unleash evil in the world. Secondly, the human heart tends toward sin and wickedness. Many blame God for the bad things that happen, but He is the cure, not the cause of evil.

In layman's terms, Satan at one time was amongst the elite of heaven. He served as the primary worship leader. He was not content with his status and wanted to be worshipped as God is. The results of his pride were not good. He was kicked out of heaven (Luke 10, Isaiah 14) but not stripped of all power. Instead, he was given the freedom to unleash his ways on earth. His evil ways are first noted in the Bible in

Genesis when he tempted Adam and Eve. His days are numbered, and he will be cast into the Lake of Fire.

Why doesn't God stop the evil in the world? Simply put, God has given us free will to make the right choices. We are all born as sinners and fall short of the glory of God (Romans 3:23). That predisposes us to sin (to do and think wrong things). It is the power of Christ in us that allows us to turn from sin and resist the influence of Satan and our thoughts and desires. Not only can you resist your temptations to do evil, but you can become an influencer of good, not evil. Just as evil speech and actions beget more of the same, true positive speech and actions snowball in society and begin to hold back the tide of evil.

You can help stop the evil around you. Am I saying that you have the power to stop the evil in the world completely? No. Evil will continue to exist until the second coming of Christ (John 14:1-3) when Jesus Christ returns, and Satan is cast into the Lake of Fire (Revelation 20). You do have the ability to turn back the actions on a local or regional level, or if your platform of influence is large enough, you may have a more global impact. Start small. Represent good on your local school board. Work in the political arena to demolish evil legislation and propose positive reform. Start a neighborhood crime watch. Mentor inner-city youth who know nothing except a life of crime and violence. Be positive in a world filled with evil. The 'power of Christ' that we need comes from the indwelling of the Holy Spirit, given to us when we accept Christ as our Savior.

Prayer: *"Dear God, please give me the right perspective of all that is going on in the world. Help me to remember you have given the Holy Spirit, who gives discernment and insight into the evil around me. Help me be strong and courageous and stand up for righteousness in my sphere of influence."*

~10~

Let Go of Past Mistakes

Romans 8:1 (NKJV), *"There is therefore no condemnation to those who are in Christ Jesus, who do not walk according to the flesh, but according to the spirit."*

We all make mistakes, but not all mistakes carry the same level of consequence for the mistake. There is no one reading this that has not made regret-filled mistakes. Most mistakes result from poor choices made in response to life circumstances.

With or without Christ, consequences are inevitable when a mistake is made. Typically, the bigger the mistake, the bigger the consequence. Christians are not exempt from paying the consequence, even when unintentional errors are made. You may be reading this as you are reaping the consequence of earlier actions. I want to give you hope at the beginning of this article by letting you know that God is a God of redemption. He will use your situation for good if you let Him. He will help you overcome.

The key to overcoming the consequence of past mistakes and preventing future mistakes is discovering what led you to make a mistake and how to prevent a re-occurrence People who do not know Jesus Christ as Lord and Savior are subjected to merely the psychological process of behavior modification. At the same time, those with a personal relationship with Christ can tap into the power of the Holy Spirit to assist in changing behaviors and overcoming mistakes.

Seven Steps to Overcoming the Consequences of Past Mistakes

1. Identify the problems that have resulted from the mistake(s). List them out so you can look at them in black and white rather than letting them rumble in your thoughts. The enemy of your soul (Satan) will try to keep you fearful of what lies ahead. God is merciful. No fear. Just list out the realities.

2. Take responsibility and accept that you made the mess and need to fix it. Taking responsibility and confessing your wrongdoing brings freedom and allows you to regain control over your emotions. Satan will try to bring condemnation, but the Lord says there is no condemnation! 3. Remember what you still have. You may have lost a business, a marriage, or a child. You may be facing jail time; you may have to sell a home to pay restitution for your actions. Make a list of every positive and good thing you still have. Not one or two. Keep praying and writing until you have at least ten positives on your list.

4. Trust the Lord. If you repent, God remembers your sin no more. You are not finished and God is not

finished with you. He loves you. He will use your mistakes to bring spiritual growth in your life and in the lives of others if you are willing.

5. Ask yourself hard questions. While you should not dwell on the mistakes, there are productive benefits to reflecting for a moment. Ask "What went wrong?" "What will I do next time?" "What lessons can I learn from this?" Answering these questions puts you on the offense against the devil who comes to steal, kill, and destroy you. (John 10:10) This is an important part in overcoming consequences because it gives you the ability to reflect and determine never to repeat the mistake, setting you up to move forward.

6. Remember that your mistakes do not define you. You are not the sum of your mistakes. As a person, you are separate from the bad choices you have made. Your past does not define you. Failure is not fatal. Scriptures tell us of David, John Mark, Paul, Peter, and many others who made mistakes and had to overcome the consequences of their sin. When we think of each of these, we think of their godliness and all they did for God, not for previous mistakes made.

7. Let God continue to write your story. Overcoming is a process and a choice. Follow the steps outlined as the beginning of your next chapter. Stay in close fellowship with the Lord, the local church, and other believers in Christ. Seek counseling if needed and

find a couple of people to pray with and hold you accountable as you transform to an overcomer.

Romans 8:28 (KJV) says *"And we know that all things work together for good to those who love God, to those who are called according to His purpose."* I pray you find courage and strength in the Lord as you face consequences of your mistakes and you accept the guidance of the Holy Spirit and the love of God as you work to overcome the consequences of mistakes you have made. We serve a God who takes our defeats and mistakes and uses them for good.

Prayer: *"Dear God, thank you for giving me grace and showing me mercy. Reveal to me those areas of my past that are keeping me down and preventing me from living the life of freedom you've set before me. Thank you for the healing you provide."*

~11~

Never Too Late, Never Too Old

Galatians 5: 7-8 (NIV) says, *"You were running a good race. Who cut in on you to keep you from obeying the truth? That kind of persuasion does not come from the one who calls you."*

Are you struggling with the aging process? Do you feel hopeless or depressed at the thought of another year having come and gone without you achieving dreams you've dreamed for as long as you can remember?

It's not too late! Every day is a new opportunity for a fresh start. Maybe you are thinking, "I've already started fresh hundreds of times. Why would this time be any different?" The answer lies in finding a new strategy. Don't repeat history. If something didn't work last time, it would not work this time either.

What is your dream? Take a few minutes (or hours) to sit and reflect on what worked and what didn't work. I will give an example from my own life. I'm almost afraid to talk about this with you because I have failed before. The enemy has tried to convince me I am too old to lose the extra weight and that it's too late to make a difference in my health. As I sit and ponder and renew my determination, I reflect on what went wrong.

I was running a good race. I'd lost 14 pounds before life gut-punched me again. The enemy derailed me from many goals I set for the fall as I struggled emotionally. I stood, then fell, stood again, and fell again. I was running a good race, but the enemy cut in on me.

I have a choice to make. I can wallow in the fact it isn't probable to lose 50 pounds in the next three weeks or even the next six. However, it is possible if I set my face like a flint, to lose the weight over a period of several months. It will be an hour-by-hour battle to make the right choices. I started this afternoon by packing up all of the cookies and candies lurking in the pantry. I ate salad for lunch instead of the pasta I wanted to eat. We are going to dinner later, and I have already decided to ask for the baked haddock instead of the fried shrimp I want. Choices.

Let's talk about something besides the proverbial weight loss goals so many of us set. Do you have a dream of a particular career? Why aren't you pursuing it? Do you feel like it is too late? You're too old? I don't know how old you are, but I assure you I know many who were in their fifties and sixties when they returned to school to get the degree they've always desired. I know others who made a complete job and career change this past year, even when it made no sense. I have a friend who is getting her nursing degree, and she is fifty-two. After spending more than twenty years as a heavy equipment operator, I have another friend who is obtaining her certification as a substance abuse counselor. A male friend of mine has always dreamed of doing stand-up clean comedy and is made his debut at the age of fifty-six, after retiring from his state job.

What is it you want to do? What steps can you take this year to move toward your dreams? Do you need to enroll in an educational program? Attend a writer's conference? Find a resume writer and pursue a job change? Do you need to make an appointment to see the doctor, dentist, or counselor and address lingering issues? Decide to launch the small business you've always dreamed about?

What is it that you've yet to do and feel it is now too late to do? It's never too late, and you are never too old to pursue your dreams. Rise up, dear friend, rise up and take the first step!

Prayer: *"Dear God. Thank you for helping me to realize it is never too late to pursue the dreams that you've given me. Help me to have the courage to take the steps necessary to walk in the direction of those dreams."*

~12~
Reaching and Setting Goals

Psalm 43:5 (NIV) *"Why, my soul, are you downcast? Why so disturbed within me? Put your hope in God, for I will yet praise him, my Savior and my God."*

You may feel very discouraged about life and your ability to achieve your potential. I am writing to those of you who have decided that it is not worth setting goals because you can't ever seem to reach the goals. Maybe it's just too much effort to think about setting goals in the days of an ever-changing world. I understand first-hand the challenge of moving forward in our current situation. Nonetheless, I encourage you to take the time to analyze previous goals to determine what part of the process worked and didn't work. Put your hope in God, who has plans to prosper you and give you a hope and a future.

Surely some goals you've set in the past have worked well! What did you do differently than you did the times made a plan and the plan failed? The Lord wants you to succeed. He wants to prosper you in all your ways.

Sometimes, our plans fail for a lack of counsel, just as Proverbs 15:22 (NIV) says. *"Plans fail for a lack of counsel, but with many advisors, they succeed."*

Another set of eyes is always a good idea, and support is necessary for big and small endeavors. I've set goals in the past that seemed completely attainable and reasonable to me. I've been disappointed and discouraged when the plans didn't pan out and I was unable to reach the goal I'd set for myself. When discussing the failed plans with others, often someone would point out a critical flaw in my planning and thinking process. Had I only taken the time to seek godly counsel, I would have been able to adjust my plan and be successful.

The phrase 'many advisors' doesn't mean you ask a dozen or more people for advice, but instead, you should prudently ask two or three trusted godly advisors for their input. I'm not talking about the typical weight loss resolutions people make. I am thinking more about career moves, educational plans, geographic moves, etc. Wisdom says to seek feedback, prayers, and counsel to ensure you are setting goals that align with your gifting, your current season in life, and the directional path the Lord is setting before you.

Having a group of advisors who can continue being your prayer support team as you move forward in your plans is essential. Your enemy prowls around like a roaring lion, just waiting for the opportunity to distract you and get you off track from your goals.

To that point, if you get off-track, it's ok to make 'mid-course' corrections. The purpose of setting goals isn't to have them become a bondage to you but rather to encourage you along your path to success. If you find the specifics you wrote are no longer realistic at some point, make an adjustment.

Life happens, right? I had all kinds of plans made to achieve in 2020, and well-we all know those blew up. I made adjustments and set new goals that extended into 2021/2022. While I reached some of them, life happened again and...I had to readjust again and write them for 2023.

Does that make me a failure? By no means! I could get discouraged, but I am focusing on the positives and all that has been able to be achieved, rather than what hasn't happened. What about you? Are there things you tried to accomplish that didn't happen? I encourage you to sit down over coffee with one advisor at a time (not a group meeting) and discuss your dreams, desires, hopes, and plans. Listen to their feedback and then set some goals, ultimately setting you up for success.

Prayer: *"Dear God, thank you for providing wisdom in your Word, the Bible, to guide me. Help me to identify one or two people who can help me set achievable goals that will move me forward in the plans you have for me."*

~13~

Discover Your Purpose of Life on Earth

Esther 4:14 (ESV) she was asked, *"...and who knows whether you have not come to the kingdom for such a time as this?"*

The questions of why we exist and the meaning of life on this earth are ones most of us ask. We yearn to discover the reason why we are here and desire to know our life is significant. We all desire to know and feel there is a specific reason for us being born, especially in today's world.

To discover the purpose of life on earth, one must look at the big picture. All of us are created for God's pleasure. Humans are made in the image and likeness of God. There are multiple Bible verses to this point, including Genesis 1:27.

It brings God joy when we live our lives for Him and worship Him. Each of us is intricately designed with specific gifts and talents, and purposes for being on this earth.

Perhaps you have been taught differently. I urge you to consider the existence of life on earth. If there is no God, there is no intelligent design. If there is no intelligent design, animals, and plants would be here by accident with no purpose. It would also mean you are on earth by accident and just a random chance. That is not the case. Your life has meaning.

I don't know your circumstances, but I am sure you are here for a specific purpose. Often, we get discouraged when we face difficult times and are prone to think there is no meaning and no point in life. The opposite circumstances also lead one to question the real meaning of existing on earth. You may be successful in your career and living comfortably, yet wondering if this is all there is to the purpose of existing.

You are not here by accident. God created you in exactly this space in time, and you were born in your geographic region to fulfill a specific purpose He designed for you in your generation.

Acts 13:36 (NIV) tells us that David, one of the best-known men of the Bible, "*served God's purpose in his generation.*"

Esther is one of the better-known women of the Bible and she questioned why she had to be the spokesperson for the Jews. In Esther 4:14 (ESV) she was asked, *"…and who knows whether you have not come to the kingdom for such a time as this?"*

Your life has a specific purpose too. No one else can do what you are designed to do because you are unique. God loves unique and thoughtfully designed you.

The Bible says, *"You made all the delicate, inner parts of my body and knit me together in my mother's womb. Thank you for making me so wonderfully complex. Your workmanship is marvelous and how well I know it."* (Psalm 139: 13-14 NLT)

David had a specific purpose. Esther had a specific purpose. I've already pointed you to Scriptures in the Bible verifying you are created in God's image, uniquely designed for His pleasure, and created for a unique purpose.

Three Steps to Begin Discovering Your Purpose

1. If you are not already a part of a Bible-teaching church, join one. There, you will find like-minded Christ-followers who are intent on becoming more like Christ (remember, we are made in His image to become like Him) and desire to live with purpose. They will disciple (teach) you to help you learn more about your purpose.

2. Answer the question, "What would I do for the rest of my life if time and money were no issue and I knew I could not fail?" The answer to your question will reveal your passion. Your purpose is typically aligned with your passion.

3. Begin small and serve others. Frequently, we don't pursue passion because of time, money, and the fear of failure. Are you passionate about cooking? Maybe you can't afford to open a restaurant right now, but

could you cook meals at a soup kitchen? Can you make a meal for a new mom or neighbor living alone? Whatever your passion, find a way to begin to express it in small ways.

Prayer: *"Dear God, thank you for beginning to show me the purposes you have for my life. Help me to take small steps that will help me discover what your plan is and the courage to move forward."*

~14~

Believe God Will Help You

Matthew 7:11 (NIV), Jesus asked, *"If you know how to give good gifts to your children, how much more will your Father in heaven give good gifts to those who ask him?"*

You may have a situation in your life that seems impossible and are asking the question, "When will God help me?" You may feel despondent, lacking hope that God does hear the cry for help. God does listen to you and does hear your cry for help.

Three Ways that God Helps You

1. God provides answers to your prayers. Because He knows what is best for you (Jeremiah 29:11) and His ways are not your ways (Isaiah 55:9), the answers may not be the ones you are waiting for, but He is faithful to answer.

2. God plans to work all things together for your good (Romans 8:28). He loves you with an everlasting love. He is your spiritual Father, and His heart is toward you. Often, working all things together requires God to maneuver circumstances, wait on you to take a step in the process, or for another person in your life to take action on something.

3. God loves to help you. There is nothing He will not do to help you when you are seeking Him and living your daily life to please Him. Unanswered prayers are challenging for people of all ages, even mature Christians. C.S. Lewis, a famous author and theologian, watched his precious wife die of bone cancer. His prayers seemingly went unanswered from an outside perspective. Not necessarily.

~

Faith and trust in Christ are necessary to finding peace when God seemingly ignores prayers and it seems He does not intend to help you in your circumstances. Just as Jesus did in the Garden, each of us must learn to pray 'not my will, but your will be done' and know that God has the best plans.

Perspective can quickly become negative if you wait for Him to help you. Whether you need food, housing, finances, a job, physical healing, relational healing, or emotional healing, know that you can trust God.

Be careful not to dismiss unconventional answers to the prayers you are waiting for God to answer. While it is incredible when God steps in and supernaturally heals a person with an illness, often, the help comes through medical intervention. Help for a job may come in the form of God bringing a person across your path looking for employees. It may not be the job you were praying for, but remember that God's ways are not yours. You don't know what stepping stone a provided position may become! Suppose you pray for God to help with a strained family relationship, and a co-worker begins asking questions about your family. In that case, God probably intends to use your co-worker to help you gain perspective and partner in prayer with you.

Reading the Bible is an essential way of discovering what God says about Him being a very present help in the time of trouble. Scriptures such as Psalm 46:1 will comfort you if you trust God. The Amplified version says God is a well-proven and very present help. Let the phrase 'well-proved' sink deep for just a moment. Well-proved indicates others can testify to the fact that God has helped them. Acts 10:34 is written to remind you God is no respecter of persons. What He has done for others, He will do for you.

As previously stated, God's ways are not our ways. His timing is not ours. As you pray and wait for God to bring the help you ask for, remember He loves you and wants to provide the best for you. He is trustworthy, and help is coming.

Prayer: *"Dear God, thank you for being my ever-present help in times of trouble. Thank you for the answers to my situation. May I be reminded to keep praying and believing that your timing is perfect and that you care."*

~15~
Defeat Financial Anxieties

Matthew 6:25 (NIV) *"Therefore I tell you, do not worry about your life, what you will eat or drink; or about your body, what you will wear.*

Many people today, regardless of faith, acknowledge feeling fearful and anxious about their financial situation. There are legitimate reasons to be concerned in today's global climate. Still, the Lord does not want us to live in a state of fear and anxiety because of financial insecurity.

There is a difference between being aware and being anxious. Wisdom dictates you be aware of the global supply chain issues, diesel shortages, massive herd deaths, fires, and storms that are destroying food plants and the ever-increasing prices of goods. Wars and rumors of wars are nothing new but a person not trusting in God, the creator of the universe may feel intense anxiety over financial insecurities. More than half of those who report having fears and anxiety admit they have difficulties controlling the financial worries that plague them. I pray you are who knows that the God who cares for the sparrow and the lilies of the field will also care for you.

The more you keep your concerns and worries locked up in your mind, the higher your anxiety will be. It is important to research and get your information from reliable sources, which often exclude mainstream media as well as the Doomsday Prepper sites. Balance is the word you should remember as you stay aware of what is happening globally and in your region.

Signs of excessive anxiety and worry over finances include loss of sleep, difficulty concentrating, and overall fatigue. These signs can be wrongly attributed to a physical illness when in reality, it is a mental health issue. Our mental health impacts our physical health and left unresolved, can lead to diseases such as heart disease, ulcers, cancer, and chronic pain.

Three Steps to Take

1. Do a realistic assessment of your current financial situation. Highlight which areas you have control over. For example, you cannot control the rising cost of food, but you do have control over what you purchase with the budget you have.

2. Write a goal for each highlighted area over which you have control. For example, because you have control over which food items you purchase, your goal could be to eliminate buying junk food snacks and put the money toward more nutritious, whole foods instead.

3. Break down your list of goals into action steps. For example, one of my current goals is to combine errands into a single trip per week on Fridays.

Another is to take advantage of sales items. My action steps include creating a 'route map' for myself, looking at sales fliers during the week and listing out which stores I will visit, as well as planning to complete my errands after lunchtime so that I am not tempted to buy lunch out.

Do Not Worry

The Lord does not want you to worry about your finances but wants you to trust that He will take care of you. Slowly and thoughtfully read this passage. Matthew 6:25-34 (NIV)

"Therefore I tell you, do not worry about your life, what you will eat or drink; or about your body, what you will wear. Is not life more than food and the body more than clothes? Look at the birds of the air; they do not sow or reap or store away in barns, and yet your heavenly Father feeds them. Are you not much more valuable than they? Can any one of you by worrying add a single hour to your life? And why do you worry about clothes? See how the flowers of the field grow. They do not labor or spin. Yet I tell you that not even Solomon in all his splendor was dressed like one of these. If that is how God clothes the grass of the field, which is here today and tomorrow is thrown into the fire, will he not much more clothe you—you of little faith? So do not worry, saying, 'What shall we eat?' or 'What shall we drink?' or 'What shall we wear?' For the pagans run after all

these things, and your heavenly Father knows that you need them. But seek first his kingdom and his righteousness, and all these things will be given to you as well. Therefore do not worry about tomorrow, for tomorrow will worry about itself. Each day has enough trouble of its own."

Remember the word 'balance.' Wisdom says that you trust the Lord to provide for your needs, but at the same time, we have our part to play, just as Gideon played a part in the battle and the part Joshua played when taking the land. Our part is to prudently evaluate and take action, as listed in steps 1-3 above. May the Lord bless you and keep you, and may His face shine upon you and give you peace in the midst of the financial storm we find ourselves in!

Prayer: *"Dear God, thank you for the promises you have given. When I am feeling anxious, help me to remember that you clothed the fields and fed the birds of the air, and you will take care of all of my needs. I seek your kingdom first, and trust you with my current and future needs."*

~16~

Hope When Not with Your Loved One

John 14:27 (NIV) *"Peace I leave with you, my peace I give you. I do not give to you as the world gives. Do not let your hearts be troubled, and do not be afraid."*

Families and friends continue to struggle if being with their loved ones is not possible. Sometimes distance is a factor. Sometimes a lack of transportation is a factor. Sometimes there are restrictions from visiting a loved one in a care facility. It is emotionally taxing regardless of why you cannot be with your loved one.

We find hope in recognizing that our omnipresent God is there with our loved ones and present with us. His abiding presence is always with them and us. Knowing God is with a loved one is comforting; however, practical steps must be taken.

Even if you cannot be with your loved one during an emergency, you can be proactive with the medical team. The first step is to determine who the family spokesperson will be. Having a single spokesperson helps avoid mixed messages between the medical team and the family. If your loved one is very sick, their condition and required treatment may change frequently, and it is best to have one primary point of contact. If you are not the primary contact, be sure the primary communicates with you in a way that allows you to be peaceful in the circumstances.

The waiting period can be a time of extreme anxiety and stress. Hope is found in praying for the peace of God to flood the soul of you, your loved one, as well as your family and friends. Accept God's free gift of peace and let it create a calm spirit within you amid the storm.

Hopefully, the medical team will offer to create a way for you to see your loved one. If not, be firm about asking for the effort to be made. Audio is excellent during normal circumstances, but emotions during times of crisis are soothed with video calls. My friend was allowed to 'see' her mom daily while hospitalized. Most nurses are tech-savvy and have facility iPads available to use. FaceTime is an option for family members who have Apple devices. Zoom is another option to use across all types of devices. If your loved one cannot communicate, there is still comfort for both of you if video calling is employed.

While keeping in touch with your loved one and the medical team, it is important to practice self-care. First and foremost, you must dig deep spiritually and allow the Lord to pour into you and strengthen you. He has promised you His strength. He will not give you a trial you cannot handle with His help. Isaiah 41:10 (ESV) says, *"So do not fear, for I am with you; do not be dismayed, for I am your God. I will strengthen you and help you; I will uphold you with my righteous hand."*

Once you've had your spiritual nourishment, ensure that you eat healthy foods and give your body the physical rest you need. Even though family members are typically restricted from visiting during the pandemic, they can wrestle with guilt that they let a loved one down in their time of need. Be intentional in keeping your immune system strong, praying throughout your day, listening to Christian music, and intentionally engaging in physical activity to decrease the stress in your body.

Prayer: *"Dear God, thank you for your watch-care over my loved one. I am thankful that you are omnipresent and are with them where they are and also here with me. Help me to remember to take care of myself during this current crisis in my family and to stay connected to you and my family."*

~17~
Coping During the Holidays

1 Peter 5:7 (NLT) *"Give all your worries and cares to God, for He cares for you."*

There are many holidays and family celebrations throughout the year. Having a picture perfect holiday isn't always possible.

It is important to acknowledge your feelings and even cry as you express them, as long as you don't make a daily habit of it and isolate yourself. Grief and sadness are normal feelings for many during a time of gathering and celebration, especially if someone you loved has recently died or you are distanced from loved ones for other reasons. Here are seven coping strategies that will help alleviate you keep depression and stress at bay.

7 Tips for Coping

1. Be realistic about the current circumstances. Daily life lately is anything but normal for most of us. Traditions of gathering together may not be possible for you this year for many reasons, but perhaps you can establish a new tradition together. One idea is for everyone to share a favorite meal and memories via Zoom, being sure to record the gathering. (The idea is you all make the same recipe and eat it together, each in your own house.) Now each family member will

have a precious bit of family heritage to watch over and over.

2. Consider volunteering in the community or in your local church. Soup kitchens would be happy to accept home-baked goods or special holiday side dishes if you are a person who loves to cook.

Another option would be to help box holiday meals at a local pantry or ministry and then participate in the deliveries. Nothing lifts a mood like seeing the joy on the faces of those who could not afford to buy special foods for the holidays.

3. Do something special for a friend or neighbor. Focusing on bringing cheer to others will force you outside of your situation. I make homemade chocolates and box them up to give to friends. While it is true that some people are still hesitant to accept food gifts, I've had no one turn down my delicious peanut butter balls and cracker candy.

4. Reach out to others if you are battling isolation and/or depression. Many people have added complications from a divorce or separation. Our church offers a DivorceCare ministry, which is a national ministry. DivorceCare offers a special edition called 'Surviving the Holidays.' We also offer Grief Share at our church, geared specifically for those who have experienced the loss of a spouse, loved one, or friend.

Grief Share is national and offers a 'Surviving the Holidays' session. Many of these are offered virtually now, which is a significant benefit to those who may not have a session in their local area. Online support groups through community agencies are also helpful to those who are struggling.

5. Traditions in my family aren't just for Thanksgiving and Christmas. For some people, every holiday is a reason to gather and celebrate. Don't miss out! Plan out a bucket list of how you'd like to spend the holidays to ensure days don't turn into weeks with no activities. Set aside time to shop, bake, go to a couple of parties, and visit with those friends and family you are able to. Don't forget to make a list of your favorite movies and set aside time to watch them.

6. Indulge yourself in self-care, starting with eating healthy most of the time, and allowing 'cheat times' for those special holiday foods you love. Get 15-30 minutes of exercise a day to increase the endorphins and decrease stress. Don't forget how important a good night of sleep is, but don't let the pendulum swing too far in the other direction and sleep the days away.

7. Spending time with family is important, but so is staying involved in your local church family. Sign up

for the outings. Connect with people. Pray often, and especially for others. Keeping your focus will help you maintain your joy, regardless of circumstances.

Prayer: *"Dear God, thank you for providing practical ways for me to cope with anxiety, depression, and stress during the holidays we celebrate throughout the year. Help me to practice self-care. Give me the desire and ability to connect with family and friends, whether in-person or electronically. Thank you for your love."*

~18~

Choose Kindness Over Bitterness

John 16:33 (TM) *"In this Godless world, you will continue to experience difficulties."*

If you are like most people, you are dealing with emotional pain in some area of life. Being a Christian doesn't preclude us from being subjected to the circumstances of life that cause sorrow and pain. Much as we'd like to avoid the difficulties, they rear their ugly heads far too often.

I once knew a woman who was so bitter and angry over all of life's hurts that she was just plain rude to everyone. The clerk at the grocery store became a target of cutting remarks when there was a glitch at checkout. The bank teller felt the sting of money being snatched out of her hand. Living in a small community meant that everyone knew who she was and tried to duck her when she walked toward them at the Post Office and other places. Why the bitterness?

Teen pregnancy changed the course of her life, and rather than continue to pursue her dreams as a mom; she shelved them. Every person she encountered represented a life she might have had if not for an unexpected pregnancy and marrying young. While everyone understood her pain, the unkind attitude was too much for people to handle.

Bitterness is defined as anger and disappointment at being treated unfairly or carrying the perception of being treated unfairly. The Bible says the rain falls on the just and the unjust. (Matthew 5:45). On this side of heaven, there will be many instances in life when we are rained on unjustly. It's normal to ask the 'why' questions and express anger, even anger at God for allowing such injustice.

Responses such as anger are a part of the grief cycle, and whether recognized or not, there's always a component of grief when loss happens. The key is to seek help through the grieving process and find healing so bitterness doesn't set in and unkindness.

Consider this example of someone who had every reason to be bitter yet has chosen a better way. I have a friend who was a roofer. One day two decades ago, he had a horrible accident that left him paraplegic and nearly ended his life. He's fought the onslaught of medical issues, physical challenges, and changes to his lifestyle, marriage, and family. Yet, much like Joni Erikson Tada, he continues to be a beacon of light to everyone around him. If anything, he views life as a precious gift and lives daily to the fullest, spreading kindness to those he encounters.

Another example is that of a young couple I know who has experienced the pain of child loss on several occasions. From the world's standards, it would be understandable if they refrained from interacting with other young families, given the severity of their grief. Yet, I've watched over the years as they continue attending baby showers and congratulating others as their babies are born. I've observed their choice to be kind to all of those around them while dealing with seemingly insurmountable odds themselves. They've opted to seek grief counseling and find the healing they need, which allows them to be kind to others rather than bitter.

If you struggle to be kind to others, is it possible that bitterness has started to take root in your heart? Is there a time you can recall feeling like the rain of injustice fell on you? Someone got a promotion, and you were passed by, or perhaps someone wronged you somehow?

It is impossible to demonstrate kindness at the same time as harboring bitterness. Is there someone you need to forgive? A loss you need to grieve? Your heavenly Father desires to bring healing to your heart, allowing you to genuinely show love and kindness to others. The healing process is not one I can write a formula for and not something gained from reading a quick article. While it may be the catalyst causing you to recognize there is a need, I recommend you reach out to the pastor of your local church for counsel.

Prayer: *"Heavenly Father, I pray you provide the counsel needed if there are any roots of bitterness or feelings of injustice lingering deep within that* *prohibit feelings of genuine kindness toward others. Lord, I am grateful you love each of us with an everlasting love and extend grace. May I learn to be kind enough to extend the same grace to others."*

~19~

Trust in the Faithfulness of Jesus

Matthew 24:35 (ESV) *"Heaven and earth will pass away, but my words will not pass away."*

I love the hymn "What a Friend We Have in Jesus." Do you know it? I especially love the line that says, "Can we find a friend so faithful, who will all our sorrows share?" Because we are humans, at times, we will fail our friends, and they will fail us. Recently, I failed a friend by not following up with her about her skin cancer diagnosis. Isn't it wonderful to know that Jesus does not forget, get too busy, or lack compassion in our time of need?

The Hebrew meaning of faithfulness is steadfastness, firmness, and fidelity. The opposite of faithfulness would be wavering and constant change. We know from the Bible that God (the Father, Son, and Holy Spirit) are unchanging God is faithful.

As you get to know God and His character better, you will recognize His faithfulness in your life, in the big things and the small. Studying the Bible will reveal a pattern of His faithfulness throughout the ages. The Lord cannot and does not lie (Numbers 23:19), and what He says will come to pass. When you read in Isaiah 43:2, He will be there as you walk through the waters and fire; you can trust His faithfulness. He is no respecter of persons (Acts 10:34), so what He has done for others, including me, He wants to do for you.

Matthew 24:35(ESV) says, *"Heaven and earth will pass away, but my words will not pass away."* That passage means exactly what you think it means. The words spoken by God, found in the Bible, will not change and will not cease being valid, even though this earth will (and the new earth comes to be).

We can trust in the faithfulness of God, in the person of Jesus, when we need healing. Psalm 147:3 tells us Jesus heals the brokenhearted. Matthew 9:35 tells of Jesus going village to village, healing every manner of sickness and disease. Whether we need healing in our spirit or physical body, Jesus cares and is faithful to heal.

Think back over the past year, then the past decade, and then back over the years since childhood. As you reflect, make a note of all of the times God has come through for you. Remember that often those needs have been met through people that God has put in your path. Can you recall when you had a financial need, and someone blessed you with money or food? When you were so downcast and discouraged, and a friend dropped by for coffee and spent time encouraging you? These are demonstrations of how God faithfully meets our needs.

God always hears you (1 John 5:14, Psalm 34:15), always supplies your needs (Philippians 4:19), and loves you with an everlasting love (Jeremiah 31:3). He who started a good work in you is faithful to complete it (Philippians 1:6). What do you need from God today? Whatever the need, you can trust that God is faithful. Bring your requests before the throne and know that Jesus hears you and is ever-interceding on your behalf to God the Father (Hebrews 7:25).

Prayer: *"Dear God, thank you for your faithfulness and the reminders today of how much you care about me. Thank you for all of the times you have met my emotional needs in the past and for the times you will in the future. Help me to remember these things as I trust you in the midst of difficult times."*

~20~
God Forgives You

As humans, we are prone to sin daily. For some, the sin is seemingly insignificant and of no consequence, while for others, the sin is 'a big one'. The question of "Could God ever forgive me" looms in the mind of many of us when we fail. The short answer is yes; God loves you and will forgive you.

The grace of God is limitless. Nothing you have ever done or will ever do is not forgivable. Furthermore, there is no sin that is bigger than another. All wrongdoings are considered sin, and according to Romans 3:23, all of us have fallen short and have sinned. The small white lie is just as sinful as committing a criminal act.

Whatever you have done wrong or are considering doing even today has not surprised God. He created you and knows you, and loves you despite wrong actions or thoughts. He will forgive you. When Jesus died on the cross, it was for all of your sins. Not some of them. Not just the little ones. All of them! You cannot out-sin His grace. God can forgive you of everything, big and small.

You may be wondering how a perfect God can forgive egregious sins. Consider the story of the two thieves on the cross and the conversation that took place as Jesus hung on a cross in between them.

(Luke 23:32-43 NIV) One thief mocked and scorned Jesus as they all hung there dying. The other recognized his own sin and admitted guilt. Jesus then looked at Jesus and said, *"Remember me when you come into your kingdom."* Jesus immediately forgave the thief who had repented and said in verse 43, *"Surely today you will be with me in paradise."* Even in the last moments of life, sins can be forgiven if a person truly is sorry (repentant) and believes in Christ.

God doesn't merely 'decide' to forgive you of your sins as if the answer could either be 'yes' or 'no', and at any moment, He would change His answer to stop forgiving people if His mood changed. It isn't a mere dismissal of sin from the judge of heaven and earth. God is justice and must follow through on His Word, which says that Jesus paid the debt for everyone. The ransom has been paid, in full, now and forevermore. Your sins have been justified, now and forevermore. Not because of anything you have done but because Jesus fulfilled God's requirements and became the perfect, sinless 'lamb of God.'

Jesus is the only man to have ever lived the perfect life, able to do so because while He came to earth in the form of flesh and was fully man, He retained being fully God and was incapable of sin.

He understands you because while fully man, He felt the range of emotions and experienced the challenges you face. The Bible says in Hebrews 4:15 that Jesus was tempted and yet without sin. Because he lived a sinless life, God the Father accepted His son Jesus' death on the cross as having paid the required sacrifice that guarantees forgiveness for everyone, with one stipulation.

God will forgive you for your sin, but you must do your part. You need to be in a personal relationship with Jesus before God extends grace to you and offers forgiveness.

You must believe that God loves you so much that He sent His son, Jesus Christ, to pay the penalty for your sin (The wages of sin is death-Romans 6:23). You must honestly believe Jesus is the Son of God who came to earth and lived a perfect, sinless life, died on the cross to pay for your sin, was buried, then rose again on the third day.

Confessing with your mouth what you believe in your heart is the first step in becoming a Christian who has a personal relationship with Jesus. Then you can pray to God, asking Him to forgive you of your wrongdoings. He is a just God, and he will forgive you because you are in a personal relationship with His son Jesus, who paid it all for you.

If you continue to feel as though you are not forgiven, seek out a pastor or pastoral counselor who can help you more fully understand the finished work of Jesus on the cross and help you learn to accept the free gift God has given you by forgiving you of all you have ever done or ever will do as you live an imperfect life here on earth.

Prayer: *"Dear God, thank you for making a way for my sins to be forgiven. Help me to know and feel that forgiveness."*

~21~

Be Thankful in All Things

1 Thessalonians 5:16 (NIV). *"Give thanks in all circumstances; for this is the will for you in Christ Jesus."*

Maybe it's been a hard year and you have had to deal with so much pain and loss over these months. You may not be feeling thankful about anything happening in life right now. You could have thoughts running through your mind such as I know I am supposed to be thankful for everything. Should I be thankful for losing my job? How can I be grateful when my loved one passed away? Do I really need to be thankful when I am estranged from my family?

It is a normal response to find it difficult to count blessings amid the pain of life. Yet, giving thanks in all things is just what we are directed to do.

The directive is to give thanks in all circumstances, yet many interpret and quote this passage as saying 'give thanks for all circumstances.' These two words carry very different meanings and make all of the difference as you express your gratitude to God.

Despite how difficult the year has been and how dire the circumstances are, we can still express thankfulness to God. Not for our circumstances, but for God being who He is and all of the blessings He has bestowed upon us.

Perhaps you've suffered tremendous financial loss. You may have bill collectors calling your phone daily and no answers on when you can make payments. Has the Lord taken care of you? In what ways has He blessed you? Perhaps you've accessed a local food pantry, or someone provided groceries for you. Can you recall the unexpected sale you found on those items you needed? You can thank God for all the blessings He has given during your time of hardship. Biblically speaking, you don't need to thank him for the circumstances but for the ways you've been blessed.

Many of us have suffered the loss of loved ones. The Lord would never expect you to be thankful for those losses. Again, the key is to find the blessings in the midst of grief and loss. Perhaps someone has cooked meals and brought them to your home. Maybe you've received a flood of sympathy cards and notes. Did someone come alongside you and hold your hand or text you daily? Express your thankfulness to the Lord for the acts of kindness.

Should you be thankful for an estranged relationship? By no means! You can, however, express your thankfulness to the Lord for sustaining their lives and surrounding them with His presence and continue praying for healing to come into the relationship.

Ponder for a moment the attributes of God, all He has done and is doing for you. You will be able to thank Him in your circumstances because He promises never to leave or forsake you. His eye is upon you. The righteous are never forsaken and left begging for bread. His eye is on the sparrow. Weeping may endure for a nighttime, but joy comes in the morning.

Prayer: *"Dear God, thank you for showing me all of the blessings you have given me in the past. Thank you for reminding me that I should be thankful in all things, but do not need to be thankful for all things. Help me to trust you in the midst of my circumstances and to remain grateful and thankful for the ways you care for me."*

In closing…

We have come to the end of our 21 day journey together. It is my prayer that your mental well-being has improved over the past three weeks and that you have discovered some new strategies to implement to keep your mental health at an optimum level. None of us go through life without days of struggle, but implementing the strategies listed out over the 21 days will help you rebound faster than you typically do.

Meanwhile, I've added bonus material and a list of resources that you may find helpful.

If you find yourself still struggling, reach out to myself or your local pastor. I'd be happy to talk to you about some next steps.

Blessings to you,
Mel

Bonus Material

Questions Often Asked by People Experiencing Anxiety in This Chaotic World

~Q1~

Do I Have to Clean Up My Act First?

Billy Graham was a famous preacher and evangelist, known world-wide. He preached over 400 times in 185 countries, speaking to more than 200 million people. Each time he ended a service, he gave an invitation for people to receive Jesus. The old hymn played in the background, inviting people to come to Christ just as they are. God does not expect people to clean up their act before becoming a Christian. When people accept Christ as their Lord and Savior, changes begin as the Holy Spirit works in them.

Verse two of the hymn says "Just as I am and waiting not, to rid my soul of one dark blot. To thee whose blood can cleanse each spot, Oh Lamb of God, I come." Maybe you are have more than one dark blot, more than one mistake that you've made. Maybe you wonder if Jesus will really forgive what you have done. He will. You do not need to clean yourself up before becoming a Christian. He loves you, just as you are.

In Matthew 12:31-21, we are told Jesus forgives all sins, except the sin of blaspheming the Holy Spirit; that is to say you have deliberately and repeatedly hardened your heart against God. If you believe in

Jesus and believe He died to forgive you of all of your sins past, present, and future; your sins are forgiven. (Romans 10:9)

We need the power of the Living God, in the form of the Holy Spirit that lives inside of us, to clean us up and make us new. Don't try to clean yourself up before deciding to become a Christian. You cannot do it in the power of your own strength and self-will. If you were able to clean yourself up, you would have done it already.

Come broken, and the Lord will mend you. Come with all of your emotional wounds, and be healed. Do you need to be rescued? He is your rescuer. Are you empty inside? He will fill the void in your life? Are you struggling with a load of care, burdened by all you are dealing with? He is your burden bearer. He sets the captive free, breaks the bondages that keep you from freedom. Are you overwhelmed with guilt? He is the one who pardons you. These are all promises found in the Bible.

The Bible also says you shall know the truth and the truth will set you free. (John 8: 31-32) Jesus is the way, the truth, and the life. The more you get to know him, through reading the Bible and spending time with him in prayer; the more you will desire to change. You will be 'cleaned up' and become more like Jesus as time goes by.

Some people describe the decision to let Jesus clean you up as a 'Come to Jesus Moment'. You don't need to be in a church service. You can make that decision wherever you are right now as you read this. My come to Jesus moment took place in my living room while reading a book written by Billy Graham entitled 'You Must Be Born Again'. You are loved just the way you are. You don't need to get rid of bad habits or somehow fix past mistakes or clean yourself up before beginning your life as a Christian. You can make that decision today, just as you are.

~Q2~

Why Is There Evil in the World?

We are living in a world filled with all sorts of evil including crime, war, terrorism, racism, and all manner of societal woes. The snowball effect occurs as evil happens and incites yet another act of evil and hatred. As things intensify, many are asking why evil is in the world.

Evil exists in the world because of two primary sources. The devil (referred to as Satan hereafter) is a primary source and has free reign to unleash evil in the world. Secondly, the human heart tends toward sin and wickedness. Many blame God for the bad things that happen, but He is the cure not the cause of evil.

In layman's terms, Satan at one time was amongst the elite of heaven. He served as the primary worship leader. He was not content with his status and wanted to be worshipped as God is. The results of his pride were not good. He was kicked out of heaven (Luke 10, Isaiah 14) but not stripped of all power. Instead, he was given the freedom to unleash his ways on earth. His evil ways are first noted in the Bible in Genesis when he tempted Adam and Eve. His days are numbered, and he will be cast into the Lake of Fire, but for now, he has free reign on anyone who does not invoke the power of the Living God to stop the evil.

The story of Adam and Eve is one most of us know. Satan disguised himself as a snake and convinced Eve to eat the forbidden fruit. The action of eating the forbidden fruit allowed sin to enter the human heart for the first time. We now have to contend with our hearts as well as the hearts of others, and the evil that comes from it. You may think you are a good person, certainly compared to 'fill in the blank'. Yet, the Bible is clear that all of us are plagued with the same issue. Jeremiah 17:9 (ESV) says "The heart is deceitful above all things, and desperately sick, who can understand it?" Other translations say 'desperately wicked' rather than 'desperately sick'.

Why Doesn't God Stop the Evil in the World?

Simply put, God has given us free will to make the right choices. We are all born as sinners and fallen short of the glory of God (Romans 3:23). That predisposes us to sin (to do and think wrong things). It is the power of Christ in us that allows us to turn from sin, to resist the influence of Satan and our thoughts and desires. Not only can you resist your temptations to do evil, but you can become an influencer of good, not evil. Just as evil speech and actions beget more of the same, it is likewise true positive speech and actions snowball in society and begin to hold back the tide of evil.

You Can Help Stop the Evil around You

Am I saying that you have the power to completely stop the evil in the world? No. Evil will continue to exist until the second coming of Christ (John 14:1-3) when Jesus Christ returns and Satan is cast into the Lake of Fire (Revelation 20). You do have the ability to turn back the actions on a local or regional level, or if your platform of influence is large enough you may have a more global impact. Start small. Represent good on your local school board. Work in the political arena to demolish evil legislation and propose positive reform. Start a neighborhood crime watch. Mentor inner-city youth who know nothing except a life of crime and violence. Be positive in a world filled with evil.

~Q3~

Is There Life After Death?

Is there life after death and does it matter if you believe there is, or not? A quick Google search gives a variety of answers, but it does not escape my notice that none of the answers offer hope and joy to the reader.

The medical community offers no explanation other than the process of the body actively dying and the subsequent 36 hours of rigor mortis setting in. While you may appreciate knowing the biological process, it doesn't answer the question of whether or not there is life after death. The scientific community goes to great lengths to explain there is no probability of people having a spirit which is a separate entity from the physical body. Atheists believe humans merely cease to exist, having had no purpose for living.

The list of religions and the differences in the answers to the question of life after death is exhausting. The answer to the question can be found in the Bible, which is the Ancient Scrolls, the Word of God, given to people in an easily understood manner.

*** What the Bible says about Life after Death ***

Evangelical Christianity is not a religion but is based on relationships. Evangelicals follow the Bible as it was originally written, taking nothing out of it and adding nothing to it. The Bible speaks to all facets of our lives, but most important is the matter of eternal life.

The Bible teaches that God is the Creator of the Universe and all things in it. In Genesis 1, Scriptures clarify that Jesus Christ, the Son of God, was with God in the beginning and was later sent to earth to become payment for the sins of each of us. His birth, death, burial and resurrection fulfilled the requirement of God that payment be made so we can go to heaven after death. John 3:16 (NET) tells us "For this is the way that God loved the world: He gave his one and only Son, so that everyone who believes in him (Jesus) will not perish (die) but have eternal life."

In Mark 12:26-27 Jesus speaks in present tense and clarified that Abraham, Isaac, Jacob and others are still living, they are not dead. How can this be, when we know they all died? Paul wrote in 2 Corinthians 5:8 (NKJV) "We are confident, yes, well pleased rather to be absent from the body and to be present with the Lord." In Ecclesiastes 12:6-7 (NKJV) we are exhorted to "Remember your Creator before the silver cord is broken, or the golden bowl is broken, or the pitcher shattered at the foundtain, or the wheel broken at the well. (These speak of death-remember your

Creator before you die). Then the dust (Genesis refers to our bodies being formed from dust) will return to the earth as it was, and the spirit will return to God who gave it." In John 10:28 (NIV) Jesus said "And I give them eternal life, and they shall never perish; no one will snatch them out of my hand."

Jesus is the Only Way to Having Eternal Life in Heaven after Death

There is life after death. The Bible is filled with passages to study, confirming life after death. Many religions agree on this fact. What is not agreed upon is exactly what happens to you after death and where you will spend eternity.

Christianity is based on the Bible, which has proven true both historically and scientifically. The Bible is clear that you must have a personal relationship with Jesus if you want to spend life after death in heaven. You cannot do enough good works to get to heaven after you die, nor can you pray enough, be reincarnated enough times, or be a nice enough person. There is only one way to heaven, and it is by accepting Jesus Christ as your Lord and Savior. In John 14:6 NIV, Jesus answered (Thomas) saying "I am the way and the truth and the life. No one comes to the Father except through me." How can you be born again and come to the Father through Jesus?

In John 3:3 (NET) Jesus said "Very truly I tell you, no one can see the Kingdom of God (Heaven) unless they are born again. The Greek word 'again' means from above'. You need to be born again, spiritually speaking.

~Q4~

Why Do Christians Read The Bible So Much?

A question I am asked frequently is one of inquiring as to why Christians read the Bible all of the time. While I understand the word 'all' is not literal, I often rephrase the question and respond with four reasons why Christians read the Bible every day or a couple of times a day.

The Bible Teaches Us about God

Spending an afternoon outside pondering the wondrous intricacies should lead a person to logically conclude there is a Creator. Acknowledging that God exists is not the same as knowing God. Reading the Bible teaches us about the divine and triune nature of God the Father, God the Son (Jesus), and God the Holy Spirit. Learning about the loving and living God who created the universe makes Christians desire to worship Him and live in a manner that pleases, resulting in a life filled exceedingly, abundantly beyond what we could ask for or imagine (Ephesians 3:20).

The Bible is a Blueprint for Daily Living

Just as an architect needs a blueprint to build accurately, we need a blueprint for living our daily lives. The Bible gives a blueprint for what to eat, the need to rest, how to handle relationships, and the danger of not controlling our tongue. There are thousands of directives that give the smallest of details about daily living. Living life according to the Bible brings abundant blessings in life (John 10:10).

The Bible provides a Moral Compass of Truth

We are living in a time where absolute truth is no longer upheld in society. A glance at social media, mainstream news, or actions in the community around you will confirm the age of moral relativism. In other words, there is no right and wrong and everything is based on perspective and opinion.

The Bible is no longer looked to as the final authority of right and wrong, even in societies such as the United States that were founded on the truths of the Bible. While this may sound great in the name of progress and freedom, it creates a great deal of confusion for many. While some scoff at the thought of God setting a moral compass of truth, millions of Christians read the Bible every day, searching for truth. Jesus is the truth (John 14:6).

The Bible Helps Us to Be Strong and Courageous

We are human and when faced with difficulty, we need to be encouraged and reminded to be strong and courageous. Joshua was a warrior and a leader yet when faced with the daunting task of going in to possess the land given to the people; God spoke to him four times about being strong and courageous.

In Joshua 1:9 (ESV) God asked Joshua "Have I not commanded you? Be strong and courageous. Do not be frightened, and do not be dismayed, for the LORD your God is with you wherever you go." This verse is frequently quoted by Christians, but the previous verse gives the 'how' to be strong and courageous.

In verse 8 (ESV) Joshua was reminded of the key to finding the courage and strength to face the battle. "This Book of the Law shall not depart from your mouth, but you shall meditate on it day and night, so that you may be careful to do according to all that is written in it. For then you will make your way prosperous, and then you will have good success." The Book of the Law is the Bible.

The Life Lesson

Whether you need to know God better, basic instruction for daily living, moral direction, hope, strength, or courage; the key is to read your Bible often. Had Joshua not spent time reading the Bible 'all of the time', he would not have been able to stand in his time of trouble. The more a Christian reads their Bible and meditates on it day and night, the more prepared he will be in the hour of need.

When fear, depression, temptation, a diagnosis, or a crisis call comes, the Scriptures in the Bible will come back to mind and bring the instruction needed for your specific situation. You cannot recall what you have not first learned. I encourage you to take the time to read your Bible. Maybe not 'all' the time, but spending time reading it will equip you to live a strong, courageous, and victorious life.

~Q5~

Can a Christian Enjoy Entertainment?

There are many teachings on whether or not it is ok for Christians to enjoy entertainment. Some swing far left and say that all things are permissible (forgetting the Bible says not all things are beneficial) and some swing far right and say all entertainment is from the devil and Christians must avoid it. I tend to follow the more balanced approach.

In Exodus, God modeled having a day of rest, and commanded us to do the same. A legalistic view would be to use the day of rest to read the Bible and pray. Less legalistic views would say spending the day at the park having a picnic is permissible. More permissible views would say God created football and other sports to be enjoyed on a day of rest.

This world is hard and entertainment is a way to alleviate the day to day stress by laughing and enjoying a good movie or time with family and friends. Proverbs 17:22 says a joyful heart is good medicine. Research proves this is a scientific fact. We all need to take time to laugh and relax. Endless work and striving is not good.

Considerations in Choosing Entertainment

Learning to evaluate entertainment will keep you from making a diet of viewing or listening to things that promote emotions and desires for things God calls sin, which cause a desensitization. If we fail to discern when values being promoted in a particular song or movie do not align with the Bible, our hearts will be pulled away from God and toward the world.

I have basic questions I ask myself when considering different types of entertainment. As a Christian, I want to be sure that the choices I make are godly options.

First, I ask myself what the entertainment is glorifying. If I am listening to music or watching a show I ask myself if it promotes sexual immorality, crime, and drugs. Or, does it promote healthy relationships and family life? I choose the latter because I know that whatever I dwell on and allow to enter my mind and heart will be the things that begin to grow. I don't want things that God calls sin to be what I dwell on and allow to grow.

Another question I ask myself is whether or not the entertainment gives me any insight into the complex world we live in. I don't need to understand criminal minds, unless I am in law enforcement or forensics or am writing fiction books. In those cases, watching shows that give insight would be helpful. I love watching movies about overcoming the odds, which align with my Biblical values of being an overcomer.

There are many lessons to be learned from watching any type of sporting events and none more than watching the Olympics. The athletes are disciplined and determined, single focused, resilient, and resolved. All of us are called to have the character of the Olympic athletes because it is what separates the winners and losers on the field of life.

Finally, I ask myself if there is a task I am putting off because of the entertainment (such as video gaming). Too much of anything is bad for a person including too much entertainment. There is a time to work and a time to rest and engage in recreation and entertainment.

Proverbs 6: 6 reminds us to consider the ways of the ant and many passages in Proverbs remind us that the sluggard reaps regrets instead of a harvest. In other words, if it is good weather and time to plant the garden so you have food to eat the following winter; wisdom says stay home and work in the garden, rather than spend the weekend enjoying frivolous entertainment. It's a matter of priorities and staying balanced.

Judge Not

At the beginning of the article, I said there are many views on whether or not Christians should enjoy entertainment and if so, what types and to what extent. I urge you to not judge others' convictions and choices, just as you do not want them to judge yours.

We must each decide for themselves what is good and godly and in keeping with our Biblical convictions but take care that we don't ignore what the Bible is saying, so as to create a reason why it is ok. As for me, the fact that I am a Christian doesn't prohibit me from enjoying clean entertainment such as a football game, catching a theatre production, or going to a Christian music concert.

~Q6~

How Should I Pray for Healing?

Praying for healing is something people have been doing for centuries. There is evidence throughout the Old Testament that God has the power to heal and is pleased to do so. The New Testament is filled with passages recounting the miraculous healings Jesus did while walking here on this earth. God is still healing today, sometimes through medicine and sometimes miraculously through prayer.

Healings can be physical, emotional, mental, or spiritual in nature. There is no magical formula of how to pray for healing in a way that yields results, but there are biblical principles that are as true today as they were thousands of years ago.

Prophets of old believed in the healing power of God. In Jeremiah 17:14, the prophet Jeremiah spoke to the Lord with conviction as he said "Heal me and I shall be healed." There was no question in his mind as to whether God was able to heal. He prayed with a child-like, matter-of-fact faith and expected God to answer him.

In Exodus 15:26 (NIV), the Lord told His people "He said, "If you listen carefully to the LORD your God and do what is right in his eyes, if you pay attention to his commands and keep all his decrees, I will not bring on you any of the diseases I brought on the Egyptians, for I am the LORD, who heals you."

'I am the Lord who heals you.' What a powerful truth to stand on. God, who always speaks truth and remains the same yesterday, today, and forever. He is the God who heals you.

It is necessary to ponder the entire verse, to understand fully. God said *if* you listen carefully to God *and* do what is right in His eyes *and* keep his decrees (commandments and laws) He would pass by them and not bring the diseases to them. Although this was spoken centuries ago, the Biblical principles remain. We must love God and live holy lives and then pray in faith to believe for healing.

Healing is a Response to Faith

James 5:15 tells us 'The prayer offered in faith will restore the one who is sick and the Lord will raise him up and if he has committed sins, the Lord will restore him."

Jesus asked the blind men if they believed he could heal. (Matthew 9:28) He responded to the woman who had the issue of bleeding for 12 years, and said "Go, your faith has made you well." (Mark 5:34)

We should pray, expecting God to deliver a miracle. Just today, I read a Facebook post from a friend of mine who received miraculous healing in her knees this week. She couldn't walk, was preparing for surgery and in constant pain. One day as she prayed, God answered and the pain disappeared. She was able to walk with no supports and continues to this very moment. Her surgery has been cancelled because she has been miraculously healed.

I have another friend battling cancer who is fighting the good fight of faith, is praying, and has thousands of others praying for her healing. Yet, the Lord God has not healed her and taken this disease from her body.

Why Doesn't God Heal Everyone Who Prays in Faith?

That's an often asked question. False teachers would say if you believe enough, if your faith is big enough- God will heal you. I've witnessed many people face discouragement and lose their faith in God, just because he has a different plan for their lives. Sometimes, God's plan is to allow the natural things of this world, such as sickness and disease, teaching us lessons we would never otherwise learn.

Several people highlighted in the Bible faced similar circumstances and they were giants in the faith. They prayed for healing, yet our sovereign God had another plan. Paul had an unidentified 'thorn in his flesh' that plagued him constantly, and although he prayed for healing, God did not remove it. Job was a faithful servant and yet he suffered all manner of loss and sickness, during which time God molded and shaped him for the purposes for which he was created. Neither of these men lacked faith to believe God could heal them, but had to surrender their will to God's. If you read accounts of their lives (and many others), they continued praising the Lord and doing the work of the ministry, despite their situations.

How Then Shall We Live?

If you are willing to surrender your will to God's and allow him to teach you as you pray for healing, he will use you in the lives of others to bring hope and encouragement to others. If it be the will of God, as you pray for healing, he will heal you.

The model given to us is to pray in faith, believing that God has the power to heal and asking him to do so. At the same time, we must recognize that it is not always his plan to bring healing to our natural bodies. He does still love you and has a profound purpose for your life and for the pain and suffering you are going through.

RESOURCES

There are lots of free resources available help us develop a healthier lifestyle that will improve our mental well-being. Here are a few of my favorites:

*The 'YouVersion' App: I love the short doable Bible Plans found here, especially the 5 day ones! You can search by topic, based on where you are at mentally or spiritually on a given day or week.

*The 'One Minute Pause' App: Created by John Eldredge, author of 'Get Your Life Back' and several other books.

*Your Hope-Filled Perspective Podcast Episodes of Dr. Michelle Bengtson:
https://drmichellebengtson.com/podcast/

*Healthy Living Coach, Susan Neal. You can find all of her materials here:
https://susanuneal.com/healthy-living

*Arise Daily Devotionals, delivered right to your email each morning. These are so uplifting and only take a moment to read. Sign up here:
https://www.arisedaily.com/

*Focus on the Family website, Resources for Healthy Living:
https://www.focusonthefamily.com/resources-healthy-living/

*First Place for Health: A well-balanced approach to all aspects of life.
https://www.firstplaceforhealth.com/how-it-works/

* Faith Over Fear Podcast Episodes. Your faith will rise up as you listen!
https://www.lifeaudio.com/faith-over-fear/

*The Healthy Christian Women Podcast. The website is great, too! Access it all here:
https://www.healthychristianwomen.com/

Works by Dr. Mel Tavares

Books

Return to Eden: Exposing the Lies that are Destroying the Family, 2007 (Under birthname of MaryEllen Smith)

Healthy Living in a Toxic World, Quick Lists and Tips, 2014

Challenged: Equipping Families to Thrive in Today's Youth Culture, 2019

Lessons From the River, 30 Day Devotional, 2021

Compilations in several anthologies, including:
Dayspring's Sweet Tea Series: Comfort for Grieving Hearts, 2021

Celebrating Christmas, 2022

Discover again the Gift of Christmas, 2023

Contributing author to several websites

Podcast Guest on multiple podcasts per year

Made in the USA
Middletown, DE
19 May 2023